Harry's
Characters
Drawing Guide For
Kids

This book Belongs to : _____

Publisher Notes:

All aspect of the book including character, their names, and other
features of the property within the book are trademarked and
owned by their respective owners. Authors of this book just yearn
to develop children's talents without any harm to their property

HARRY POTTER

STEP 5   STEP 6

STEP 7   STEP 8

How to use this book

All you need is a pencil, pencil sharpener and an eraser to get started.

Each layout on the left shows you exactly how to draw the object step by step, simply follow along drawing in the area provided on the right-hand side, add each detail as show until the drawing is finished.

When you're completed, you can add your own detail as well as color it.

Let's get started 😉

HERMIONE GRANGER

STEP 1

STEP 2

STEP 3

STEP 4

Your turn to draw 😉

HERMIONE GRANGER

STEP 5

STEP 6

STEP 7

STEP 8

Your turn to draw 😉

RON WEASLEY

STEP 1

STEP 2

STEP 3

STEP 4

Your turn to draw 😉

RON WEASLEY

STEP 5

STEP 6

STEP 7

STEP 8

Your turn to draw 😉

SEVERUS SNAPE

STEP 1

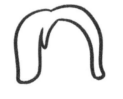

STEP 2

STEP 3

STEP 4

Your turn to draw 😉

SEVERUS SNAPE

STEP 5

STEP 6

STEP 7

STEP 8

Your turn to draw 😉

ALBUS DUMBLEDORE

STEP 1

STEP 2

STEP 3

STEP 4

Your turn to draw 😉

ALBUS DUMBLEDORE

STEP 5

STEP 6

STEP 7

STEP 8

Your turn to draw 😉

NEVILLE LONGBOTTOM

STEP 1

STEP 2

STEP 3

STEP 4

Your turn to draw 😉

NEVILLE LONGBOTTOM

STEP 5

STEP 6

STEP 7

STEP 8

Your turn to draw 😉

VOLDEMORT

STEP 1

STEP 2

STEP 3

STEP 4

Your turn to draw 😉

VOLDEMORT

STEP 5

STEP 6

STEP 7

STEP 8

Your turn to draw 😉

SIRIUS BLACK

STEP 1

STEP 2

STEP 3

STEP 4

Your turn to draw 😉

SIRIUS BLACK

STEP 5

STEP 6

STEP 7

STEP 8

Your turn to draw 😉

DRACO MALFOY

STEP 1

STEP 2

STEP 3

STEP 4

Your turn to draw 😉

DRACO MALFOY

STEP 5

STEP 6

STEP 7

STEP 8

Your turn to draw 😉

BELLATRIX LESTRANGE

STEP 1

STEP 2

STEP 3

STEP 4

Your turn to draw 😉

BELLATRIX LESTRANGE

STEP 5

STEP 6

STEP 7

STEP 8

Your turn to draw 😉

FRED & GEORGE WEASLEY

STEP 1

STEP 2

STEP 3

STEP 4

Your turn to draw 😉

FRED & GEORGE WEASLEY

STEP 5

STEP 6

STEP 7

STEP 8

Your turn to draw 😉

HARRY POTTER

STEP 1

STEP 2

STEP 3

STEP 4

Your turn to draw 😉

HARRY POTTER

STEP 5

STEP 6

STEP 7

STEP 8

Your turn to draw 😉

RUBEUS HAGRID

STEP 1

STEP 2

STEP 3

STEP 4

Your turn to draw 😉

RUBEUS HAGRID

STEP 5

STEP 6

STEP 7

STEP 8

Your turn to draw 😉

LUNA LOVEGOOD

STEP 1

STEP 2

STEP 3

STEP 4

Your turn to draw 😉

LUNA LOVEGOOD

STEP 5

STEP 6

STEP 7

STEP 8

Your turn to draw 😉

REMUS LUPIN

STEP 1

STEP 2

STEP 3

STEP 4

Your turn to draw 😉

REMUS LUPIN

STEP 5

STEP 6

STEP 7

STEP 8

Your turn to draw😉

NEWT SCAMANDER

STEP 1

STEP 2

STEP 3

STEP 4

Your turn to draw 😉

NEWT SCAMANDER

STEP 5

STEP 6

STEP 7

STEP 8

Your turn to draw 😉

LUCIUS MALFOY

STEP 1

STEP 2

STEP 3

STEP 4

Your turn to draw 😉

LUCIUS MALFOY

STEP 5

STEP 6

STEP 7

STEP 8

Your turn to draw 😉

DOLORES UMBRIDGE

STEP 1

STEP 2

STEP 3

STEP 4

Your turn to draw 😉

DOLORES UMBRIDGE

STEP 5

STEP 6

STEP 7

STEP 8

Your turn to draw 😉

MINERVA MCGONAGALL

STEP 1

STEP 2

STEP 3

STEP 4

Your turn to draw 😉

MINERVA MCGONAGALL

STEP 5

STEP 6

STEP 7

STEP 8

Your turn to draw 😉

Your turn to draw 😉

DOBBY

STEP 1

STEP 2

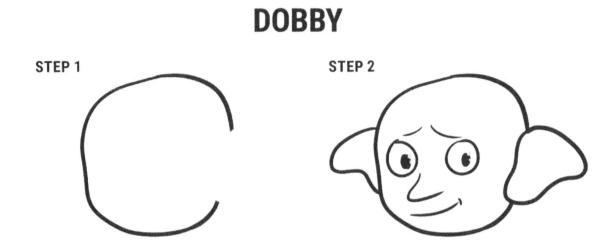

STEP 3

STEP 4

Your turn to draw 😉

DOBBY

STEP 5

STEP 6

STEP 7

STEP 8

Your turn to draw 😉

Congratulation

Now you can draw your 25 favorite Harry Potter characters, Keep practice will make you better in the drawing.

Finally, if you enjoyed this drawing book, then I'd like to ask you for a favor, would you be kind enough to leave a review for this book on Amazon? It'd be much appreciated!

Jay. T

Made in the USA
Coppell, TX
10 December 2019